# The
# Far Side of 55

A series of musings on
the human condition

by Earl F. Barfoot

Copyright © 2008 by Earl F. Barfoot

All rights reserved. Printed in the United States of America. No part of this book may be reproduced in any manner whatsoever without written permission, except in the case of brief quotations embodied in critical articles and reviews.

ISBN 978-0-557-03934-0

Graphic design and layout by James W. Barfoot

# Contents

Introduction

1. My clock was running 10 minutes fast
2. There were four boys in our family
3. It took a broken ankle
4. I've always scorned the idea of naps
5. It is with sadness that I watch my two very good friends
6. People had begun to arrive and the noise level was rising
7. I can still hear her say it: "Wash your hands …"
8. His name was Charlie
9. Over the years, I've met many people
10. This year, when I put away Christmas
11. I stood for several minutes at the door of the Chapel
12. "I've always wondered …"
13. I like the color purple
14. Every once in a while, I find a name
15. Flowers have a unique place in the gallery of gifts
16. I find April an awakening
17. There is an old saying
18. I was first introduced to yo-yos
19. It's a simple thing to do
20. One of the duties of a minister
21. When I was nearing retirement
22. I was fourth in my high school graduating class of 150
23. Yes, there was the blacksmith shop
24. I have been fascinated by shadows
25. It was a stupid thing to do
26. His eyes were full of adventure
27. You can always get my attention
28. Faith always comes wrapped in a story
29. I was fired from my first job
30. In a world of crowded schedules

31. The speaker had presented his subject clearly
32. We sometimes refer, poetically
33. The other day, I took the bus into town
34. For the first time in my life, I walked past a penny
35. I'm not a big sports fan
36. I'm a "clipper"
37. What I miss most in retirement is routine
38. I no longer put things I may frequently need
39. How did we ever allow the fork to dictate the rules
40. Sometimes I think, "There ought to be a law!"
41. We always said Grace at mealtimes
42. Time moves swiftly and you can't go back
43. I'm like Charlie Brown
44. Have you ever had your brain taken over
45. Of all the things I have heard said
46. I sometimes wonder why I am willing
47. I do crossword puzzles for relaxation
48. Other than ministers and golfers
49. I seem to be dropping things lately
50. A group of us were talking
51. This is the time of year when I get out my old coat
52. A store owner I once knew
53. We had a paper on the wall
54. Every place I have ever worked
55. If I heard it once, I heard it 100 times
56. When the American Eagle was chosen
57. The old folks used to call it "set in his ways."
58. I'm working at the fine art of waiting!
59. A hundred years ago
60. Time was, when Christmas eve saw families gathered
61. Christmas wouldn't have been Christmas
62. It's a wonderful word, "anyway" !

# Introduction

The idea for this book grew out of a casual comment. My Dad was showing the family a series of short essays he had written, and we found them charming. Someone suggested that they should be collected and published as a group; the result is the book you are now holding.

These articles were originally written one at a time, over the course of a dozen years, for my Dad's regular column in the newsletter of the Chemung County, NY chapter of RSVP. They had asked him to write commentaries about whatever interested him, and that's just what these are. Each one is a self-contained reflection on something he noticed about life and the world around him. They are sometimes about everyday experiences, sometimes reminiscences, sometimes about people he's met. Always, they are personal, gentle, and above all, life-affirming.

I have enjoyed collecting, reading, and arranging these into a book. They appear here in a sequence that vaguely suggests the progress of a year. For example, commentary describing warm-weather activities appears near the middle of the collection, winter or Christmas toward the end. This is not meant as a recommendation to read them in any particular order. They are just as much fun if you read them at random. Indeed, you will find it quite natural to read some of your favorites again and again. I know I do.

I have to say I'm really proud of my Dad. This is the man who taught me how to tie my shoes, supported and encouraged me as I learned to ride a bicycle, and showed me the how-to of many other basic skills. Always eager to discover new delights and pass them along, he was the one who first introduced me to the Beatles' music, Barbra Streisand's singing, and countless other of life's pleasures. He has always been an inspiration, a good example and model for me to follow.

As adults, we have added "friend" to our description of our relationship. Nevertheless, I couldn't resist including

this picture—one of my favorite of us together —taken on my fourth birthday when he still had about a quarter century to go before he hit the 55 mark.

Now that I've passed that mark myself, I appreciate even more the insights I find in these pages. It's a pleasure and a privilege to give the world this glimpse into his creative, positive approach to life.

Jim Barfoot

# 1.

My clock was running 10 minutes fast. I thought, "Should I turn the minute hand back 10 minutes?" "Should I stop the clock and start it again in 10 minutes when time catches up with it?" "Should I move it ahead 11 hours and 50 minutes?" "Or should I just let it go and remember that it's 10 minutes fast?"

Sometimes, especially when I'm watching the energy of children, I think I'd like to turn my life back a few years. How I'd love to recapture that moment when I hit a home run even though I had been the last kid chosen on that side. Or erase the time I broke my grandmother's mirror and lied my way out of it. Or maybe re-live those days when our kids were little and every day was an adventure with them.

But, no, that home run was a once. The mirror (if not the lie) has long since been forgotten. Our kids are all grown up and now have kids of their own.

The memories are rich but not repeatable. I am a medley of the past and present ... yes, and of the future too. Remembering is not just a yesterday thing. I am one of the many who are addicted to making lists of things I must remember to do tomorrow.

Do you know, I think I'll leave my clock the way it is, 10 minutes ahead ... or maybe more by next week. It's a reminder that time moves swiftly to create its own past. It's like having a piece of the future right on my wall. But in a strange way, it relaxes my present too.

It's nice to know that I still have 10 unused minutes before it's the time it says it is.

# 2.

There were four boys in our family. I was number three ... a set up for hand-me-downs; but that was how we had clothes. A new pair of pants was a rarity. We were lucky to have shoes that didn't need cardboard in the soles.

We were not without some extras, however. On Sundays, we all worked together preparing dinner; we each had an apron with our own name on it.

Friday supper was always fresh fish, a change from a week of rice and macaroni. Saturday movies were a nickel. My Grandma always took me. On Wednesday, my Dad filled the candy dish for the week. If it was empty before that, there was no more until the next Wednesday. It was a silent discipline to teach us to share with one another.

One day, I noticed that there was just one piece in the dish ... it was chocolates that week ... I thought I'd grab it before it was gone, so I put it in my pocket to eat later at the movies. I don't need to explain how my Mom knew what I had done.

My Mom and Dad were unequaled partners in discipline. "We'll see what your father says when he gets home", was all she said. Suppertime came and nothing had been said before or during the meal. Finally, just before the cookies were passed, my Dad turned to me, my brothers watching every move, "Earl, I'd like to speak to you" and he headed toward the back door. My mind was racing. Dad was a gentle man, but there was the woodshed, and in his hand he held a cane he had picked up. I was not reassured!

It was a clear, beautiful night. We stopped in the yard. Then Dad took my hand and with the other, pointed with his cane as high as he could reach. "Aren't the stars beautiful," he said. "God wants us all to share them. You can't put them

in your pocket." He laid down the cane and we went back inside for cookies.

    The woodshed might have been effective at the moment, but I have never forgotten the stars and Dad gently holding my hand.

# 3.

It took a broken ankle to teach me the importance of railings for up and down stairs. It took a painful few weeks with a knee that went on strike to understand why, for some of us, getting out of bed is a slower process than it used to be. When my reach isn't accurate and I tip things over or knock them off, I realize that many of the things I used to do automatically, I now have to give conscious attention, if I'm to avoid the troublesome clean-ups.

AARP sets 50 as the age of seniority, which is the polite way of saying, "growing old" ... or to soften it a bit, "growing older." I think I've been growing older for a good many years, but at least I'm not alone. The "growing older" experience is one we share in common. In a way, there's a lot of comfort in that. (I'm always surprised at class reunions to see how my friends have aged.)

But the conversations are not all "organ recitals." Nor is aging necessarily downhill. There is a certain vitality in the human spirit that allows us, with good grace, to laugh at ourselves. The things we hang onto are the feeling of dignity and worth and a sense of humor. As it takes a pad to cushion the seats of the chairs that get harder every year, so a sense of humor makes physical losses more bearable even as they become more frequent.

Listen in on any gathering of seniors and you'll pick up a funny story. Treasured companions become more delightful because we have someone to laugh with ... someone who understands from experience how important it is to cushion the day with a smile.

# 4.

I've always scorned the idea of naps. They were something for old people who had nothing to do and grew tired not doing it. "A waste of time" I thought. It was like opting out of life. The term "caught napping" was one I never wanted applied to me.

Then I saw a study of the sleep needs of college students. It recommends a short nap in the afternoon for students who are doing extra study for an exam or a class assignment. Sleep? ... in the afternoon with a term paper due? The report went on to recommend also that if you were facing a time of lost sleep, it's a good idea to take a nap before that time. And more ... experts say that a short nap in the afternoon is of more value than a few extra minutes in bed in the morning.

Well ... I know that I do run out of steam in the mid-afternoon, and it is tempting to catch a few sweet minutes of down time. But there's that prejudice, that naps are for old people (older than me, that is) ... and there's that A-type brain of mine reminding me that I have better things to do that can't be put off for nap time. Anyway, some experts warn against naps lest you spoil your night's sleep.

It was a physical therapist who solved the problem for me. While I was recovering from knee surgery, she taught me the value of putting my feet up for a few minutes each day. I soon learned that there is an instinctive connection between the feet and the eyes ... that when you put your feet up, your eyes go closed. So now I don't worry about what the experts say or about my feelings of wasting time. In the afternoon I just put my feet up.

And when I wake up, I'm ready for the rest of the day.

# 5.

It is with sadness that I watch my two very good friends growing old.

We have been together as long as I can remember. We played together in days of childhood. We went to school together and even worked together, side by side through the years. Lifetime buddies, we have been inseparable! Life has not always been easy, but we have generally managed to handle the tough times together. There have been occasions to celebrate; there have been times when we have clapped for joy over some surprising successes ... the result, certainly, of our having learned to work together so well.

It's strange, too, for my two friends are exact opposites. Sometimes this has meant that they complement each other and provide precisely what each other needs. But even when they oppose each other, it is in such a positive spirit that they seem to give each other strength through their very differences.

They have been so vibrant! It is hard to see the wrinkles appear and the arthritis begin to sap their strength. I have seen the dexterity of the one, as easily taking a pen to write a poem, as wielding a heavy hammer. The other is not quite so versatile but is still gifted with abilities that are quite unique. The one is definitely a leader; the other, more apt to play the "helper role," but still a very capable assistant. Each seems to know and accept the position that nature has assigned in making theirs an incredible partnership.

They are not just laborers and artists, however. They enjoy sports, even if not as actively as in younger days. They participate together in experiences of worship. They pull the levers in a voting machine with a sense of pride and duty of citizenship. They come together happily to recognize someone else's success. They are not afraid to get dirty in some of the grubby tasks of life.

But I especially enjoy them when they reach out to take other hands in the pleasure of friendship. How wonderful a gift they have been in my life. I thank God for my two good friends ... my hands!

# 6.

People had begun to arrive, and the noise level was rising as greetings were exchanged and conversations increased. I sat there, sipping from my glass of water. It was past time to get started. Suddenly, in a commanding voice, the chairman said, "May I have your attention." And just as quickly, the room quieted down. The meeting was underway.

I thought how important is that word that had penetrated the crowd. No communication is possible without giving attention to the speaker, no learning without the teacher's having the attention of the student. I fret over the "push the numbers" game when I make a phone call. I want attention. That's why I made the call.

There are times when we feel like saying. "May I have your attention." A little boy runs to his mother with a cut on his finger. He gets a kiss for his tears as well as a band-aid for his finger. We're all children in that we sometimes need a bandage and sometimes a kiss. How happy if we have people in our lives who can give us either one, and maybe take the time for both. And, of course, it works both ways.

In one of the nursing homes, there was a woman who had been our neighbor. I thought I'd stop and just say hello. I quickly realized that she was bursting with the need to regain the years when she was at the height of her career, and talk about her achievements. I spent an hour I didn't think I had, fascinated by her stories.

How much I would have missed if I hadn't allowed her to capture my attention!

# 7.

I can still hear her say it: "Wash your hands ... and your arms ... **and your elbows!**" Inspection before supper included all three, with particular attention to the elbows.

"Out of sight, out of mind" I thought. My elbows were behind me. Who was going to notice them? It takes a mirror for me to look at them ... "**Wash**" my mother said! Grandma was a lot easier. Living on a farm, she knew that little boys couldn't run to the wash house every time they got a little dirt on them.

I remember Grandpa when he came in to supper, though. He would roll up his sleeves and lather his arms all the way above his elbows. Then he would cup his hands in the washbowl and lift the water to his face. When he was finished, he emptied the basin on the ground ... and spit, as if to put an exclamation mark on the thorough job he had done.

Much as I respected my Mom's mandate, it was Grandpa's example that influenced me more. It seemed very adult to lather up that way, like a doctor scrubbing for surgery. And there was an intriguing parallel. Ready for the table, his place at the head was always set to include a carving knife.

I've worked at many jobs ... at a gas station, a meat packing plant, and a can factory, as well as in my own garden, all of which require scrubbing up after work. Instinctively, I wash my elbows, dirty or not; and still imitating my grandfather, I lather up, as much for the macho feeling, as for getting clean. And then I discretely spit! That's required to finish the job!

I know it's socially correct not to put my elbows on the table, but sometimes I forget, and when I do, I find myself instinctively checking for dark spots where my elbows have rested on the tablecloth.

That voice is like a recording in my head ... "Wash! ... **and your elbows!**"

# 8.

His name was Charlie. Probably in his early sixties, he had lived alone since his wife had died some five years earlier. Charlie owned and operated a small dairy farm, twenty head of cattle, and almost as many cats.

It was from Charlie that I learned the word "chores"... milking to do morning and evening, butter to churn for the next day's delivery to his customers, wood to chop for the parlor stove, hay to fork into the mangers ... the list went on and on, the things that had to be done each day before any other work could be undertaken.

In his steady, get-the-job-done way, he took care of the chores without complaining, though he sometimes fretted when they took a little more time than usual, when other tasks were demanding his attention.

But there was another word I learned from Charlie. He would speak of his "chores" and his "cheers." Cheers, like a pound of butter for Mrs. Murphy when she didn't have the money, a toy from his attic for the Jones kids when they were sick, a simple note of thanks to the driver of the snow plow, for carefully missing his mail box. "Just as important every day as Chores," Charlie would say.

"If you live with cows, you know what they need. It's the same with people. I sing to my cows, why not to my friends!" Perhaps that's a crude way to put it, but his words were defined by his actions. His "cheers" were just as important a part of his daily life as were his "chores".

Sometimes, when the deadlines approach, writing a column like this can feel like a chore. But I would rather live by inspiration than by deadlines, and when I have a story like Charlie's to share, writing becomes less like work, and more like singing a song.

Cheers!

# 9.

Over the years, I've met many people. Some have been flash experiences, like the twenty-minute conversation I had with the great writer, Isaac Asimov, a treasured moment never to be repeated. Some have been close companions with whom I have walked a short distance in a common experience and have never seen again. Some have been partners over extended periods of time with whom I have shared a vision and worked to achieve significant goals. Some have been life-long friends who have moved in and out of my life without losing the continuity of a relationship we both value.

Once in a while, I have met someone whom I have never seen before, but whom, it seems, I have always known. There is an immediate acceptance both ways, a kind of warm humanness that is comfortable for both of us. There may be specific reasons to be in contact.... an item of business, an event in which we both have a responsibility, a meeting of a group in which we both have membership. Yet, beyond that, there is a bit of mystery, a base of mutual friendship that makes each of those contacts a pleasant one.

These are the persons who add quality to my life, just by being there as a bright spirit in the mosaic of my days. These are the persons who smile with their voices and, even in their busy moments, open a space for me in their time. These are the persons who have an aura of geniality and in whose presence I feel a new surge of life in myself. If you are one of them, you may not even be conscious of it. That would be like you. But I am eternally grateful for your nourishment of my spirit.

# 10.

This year, when I put away Christmas, I took time to look through what we call our "Treasure Box." In the box are cards and letters that we have saved, year after year. It's a random collection of memories.

Each piece I picked up opened up a whole scenario ... the announcement of the birth of a son to a niece who had been abused in a first marriage and was beginning a new life with a husband with whom she has since had a happy 25-year marriage ... and family. I rejoiced for her.

There was a note from a woman who had sent me a check that made it possible for me to complete my work at Colgate-Rochester Divinity School. I had met her only once ... a long, wonderful visit. I thanked God for her.

A letter from our daughter who later died a lingering, painful death. The love she expressed, in her own handwriting, was like holding her in my arms again. I bathed her lovely spirit in my tears.

I spent an afternoon. It could have been a week, reliving the times my life has been blessed with beautiful persons. I decided that my Lenten journey this year would be a handwritten note each day to someone with whom I have been close ... family or friend ... expressing my appreciation for the way in which they have touched my life. Through the days of Lent, I want to wrap up all the difficulties and struggles, all the joy and achievements that surface from these remembrances and lay them on the altar as a package ... an offering to God.

And then I'll be ready to greet the Easter dawn with a Hallelujah in celebration of the resurrection and renewal that God's love brings to all our lives.

# 11.

I stood for several minutes at the door of the Chapel, not wanting to disturb him. He was kneeling silently in front of a picture of Jesus. Mike was known as the town drunk. This was a very different person from the man I had seen some Saturday nights after he had blown his paycheck at the local tavern.

I decided not to interrupt. He had his own personal reason for being there on his knees. If he wanted to talk with me, he would call me as he had often done before. It was not for me to intrude on this moment.

I had dreaded those calls. Mike was twice my size and brutally strong. I never was afraid of him, but he might take hours of my time and there was no dismissing him until he was ready to leave. He never knocked, so we never locked. He would have broken the door down if he decided he wanted to come in.

Now, for the first time since I had known him, I saw in him the human yearning, the searching for something that he wanted in his life and didn't know how to find. It was humbling for me to see this man who was so aggressively dominant in every situation, on his knees. I felt guilty that in my impatience with his use of my time, I had never understood his need for a redeeming faith.

Something had happened inside him. He now made a real effort to be sober when he came to see me. And we talked.... and it didn't matter that the hours went by. Alcohol was still his master, but there was something new in his life that I had not seen before. And there was something new in my life that I had not known before. Mike had experienced a kind of renewal. And now, as I walked home with him each time he came, I too experienced a resurrection.

# 12.

"I've always wondered...." How many times have I said that, or heard it from someone else! There are mysteries that we live with, that keep us asking questions, trying to figure out how and why things happen as they do.

Some are foolish little occurrences like "I wonder why the phone always rings just as I'm out the door, late for an appointment." ... or ... "I wonder why my nose always itches when my hands are in the dishwater." Little annoyances, but why do they happen again and again, I wonder.

There are the times when our imaginations soar, to take us where we cannot go. I wonder, for instance, what it would feel like to spread my wings, catch the updrafts and just lazily float on the air. And sometimes, I wonder, "Who walked this ground 100 years ago?" ... 1,000 years ago? ... long before I presumed to call it mine.

Some are the major mysteries that I enjoy letting my imagination play with. How was I formed, to be who I am? No, don't give me all the charts and diagrams and scientific studies of genes. Don't involve me in the useless debate over Creationism and Evolution. There are some things that I enjoy wondering about that never will have final answers.

If there are no mysteries, there is no wonder in life and by extension, no reverence for life. Yes, there are the little annoyances that we can't explain, that simply seem to reflect the perverse nature of things, and I laugh about them because they really have no effect on my life.

But there are the deep mysteries of life that stretch my imagination and give me hours of pleasure because they invite my spirit into places where I have never been, to see things that no one has ever known, to construct my view of and my place in my world.

My mortal limitations require that I live a "real" existence, but how empty that would be if it were not enriched by times when I can lose myself in wonder, and know that I am more than a name and social security number.

# 13.

I like the color purple. When I was 9 or 10 years old, I was given a knitted hat ... color purple ... that I loved and wore everywhere, even to bed sometimes if I didn't get caught. It came to be part of my head. I felt undressed without it. Often, I would forget that I had it on. I was constantly being reminded "Take your hat off at the table." ... good table manners being more important than being comfortable, I thought.

Even today, anything colored purple brings back that feeling of warmth and comfort that I knew with my old friend. I no longer have the hat, of course. After several years, my Mom declared it no longer washable, and it disappeared. I now have a favorite sweater, however, a deep, rich purple. A closer friend I could not have. It's even better than the hat. It's warm and comfortable, and I can even wear it at the table and still be within the bounds of good manners.

So many times, a color, or a smell, or a sound carries with it the association of a possession or an experience of the past. It may be a pleasant or unpleasant reminder, but it is an emotional attachment that never surrenders. The smell of hot metal puts me back in the factory where I worked all day with that acrid smell in my nostrils. Popcorn is still a reminder of those Sunday evenings of my childhood, sitting around the wood-burning stove in my grandparents' parlor.

I find the idea of association a very useful one today, for I have discovered that whenever I am feeling blue, I can wear something purple and feel warm and comfortable, and all's right with the world again.

# 14.

Every once in a while, I find a name running through my head ... the name of someone I haven't seen or even thought of in many years. Now, how did that name pop into my head; where did it come from so suddenly and unexpectedly?

Just the name triggers many memories of a person I once enjoyed knowing. How could I have set aside for so long, the name and face that now takes full possession of my mind? We are silent companions again, maybe for the whole day, as I reflect on the things we enjoyed doing together. The presence is so strong, my first impulse is to try to get in touch and catch up with each other ... but where would I begin? We had completely lost each other long ago. Anyway, maybe it's better to appreciate them for who they were for me at the time, and not lose the aura of that relationship.

There are so many from my past whose memories have been dimmed by the dynamics of the intervening years. I'd have to keep a book of many pages if I remembered them all. Yet, it's a delight to have one step out of the shadows and surprise me sometimes. Their tracks have not been erased. For the moment, they are uncovered and I eagerly follow where they lead, until they fade again.

I marvel at the capability of the brain to hold these beings in limbo and yet bring them forth so alive on recall. I treasure each such experience, for I am reminded again and again how blessed I have been with friendships. More than that, I find that as I recover those days with old friends, I recover a part of my own life as well.

# 15.

Flowers have a unique place in the gallery of gifts. They are sweeter than chocolates and they last longer; they smell prettier than jewelry and they are more visible; they are more immediate than books and more easily shared with others.

Yet, there's something that a single rose can do that even the most elaborate bouquets cannot. A room may be so filled with flowers that they preempt the one they honor. They are beautiful, no question about it. And for those of us who have bought flowers to send to a wedding or a funeral, we know they also carry the distinction of being expensive.

Surely, the first impression of a large display is breathtaking. I have seen people stand admiring a basket or vase, only to move on to the next, exclaiming that each is more beautiful than the others. Yet, each arrangement is soon dissolved in the total montage of floral abundance. It is like a photo which deliberately shoots the foreground sharply, leaving all that is in the background a little out of focus. It is not possible for any one flower to claim preeminence. Not so, with a single rose. It stays in focus. It is not lost in the many; it stands by itself in its own aura.

I love flowers. A pretty bouquet may fill a room with brightness. I enjoy a vase of flowers on the dining room table. But a rose becomes a silent companion as it unfolds its petals and presents a new face every day. A rose on a stand in a sick room takes up little space and can be placed within easy sight and reach of the patient. I have taken more than one person a single rose in a bud vase as a birthday greeting, a thank you, or a bit of cheer in their loneliness. I have placed many a rose on the desk of a receptionist or secretary who has been exceptionally helpful. It costs little more than a card and is more exciting.

A single rose, with a simple message … "You are special." That it can be a gift for any occasion, or no occasion, and often speaks its own message to a need we may not even know, makes it an eloquent emissary. And when you give someone a rose, add the nice touch of surprise!

# 16.

I love April. Just the sound of the word is like the tone of a lovely bell.

April comes gently, like the first rays of dawn, sending fingers of light through the weariness of March, brushing the white canvas of winter with its strokes of graceful color.

The aromatic sweetness that permeates my sleeping senses rolls back years of my life. I feel the stirrings of the earth, the freshness of the rain, and I am caught up in the joy of a world re-born. All the windows are thrown open to air out the long weeks of confinement. The sunlight that lengthens each day gives me bonus hours in the evening. I am beckoned outdoors. It is still sweater weather, but I don't mind. I enjoy sweaters; they are like hugs that embrace me with comfortable warmth in the coolness of the air.

April is a month of anticipation. The earliest flowers, struggling to break through to become part of the resurrection, give promise of more ... much more ... in May. The buds on the trees, pregnant with expectancy, remind me of a dress rehearsal, the drama to be played out as the summer unfolds. I have known the scenario many times, yet I am eager again to be in the audience as the performers turn the stage into a backdrop of luxurious green.

When I was a child, the seasons came and went, flowing continuously like a movie on the screen. With the passing of years, and the accumulation of memories, the divisions become more pronounced, each season with its own reasons for anticipation or apprehension. But season after season, it is Spring that continues to receive the warmest welcome. And April is its host.

I find April an awakening, a singing voice after a long pause in the music. I regret that it lasts only 30 days. Couldn't we at least make it one of the 31-day months?

# 17.

There is an old saying, "If you hold a bird tightly in your hand, you may imprison it, but you will not own it. If you release it and it returns to you, it is yours."

Lesley and I made a solemn promise long ago, to each other, that we would never end a letter to any of our children saying, "why don't you write?" When they were tree-climbing age, and began to scale those higher branches, I would watch and pray, "Lord, please, you take care of them; you're closer to them than I am

Not that we never gave them any warnings. Indeed we did! But we had to learn, sometimes the hard way, to adjust our rules to their growth in personality as well as their physical development as they took on more and more independence. Our oldest son rightly said to me one day as I was attempting to impose on him my point of view and not seeing his, "Dad, you're you and I'm me. If we want to continue to relate to each other, please remember that."

I drove our younger son to his first day on a college campus and helped him carry his things to his dorm room. He walked back to the car with me to say good-bye ... and I broke. He was not embarrassed; he simply smiled and said, "I understand." We both recognized that my tears were an acceptance of an adjustment that I must make in my life to accomodate the change in his.

It's not easy to open your hand sometimes. You can never be 100% sure of your bird. But I believe we have been rewarded by freeing our children and relishing the times they return to us.

I want to treat my friends the same way, to enjoy them for who they are; and to experience the newness in them each time we meet.

And even though I may misplace my trust in people sometimes, I would rather live believing in them, and watching them fly, than to tighten my hand and only know the frustration of their beating wings.

# 18.

I was first introduced to yo-yos when I was a teenager. Everybody was doing it! There were even expert yo-yo-ers performing in store windows to attract attention to the merchandise displayed beside them.

I was pretty good at the up and down thing. I even got so that I could turn the yo-yo over my hand and bring it up again. It was the more complicated maneuvers that I never mastered ... the "skin the cat", the "round the world" ... and other tricks like those. I've seen several years fly by since my teens. I don't think I have had a yo-yo in my hands in 50 years. But I can still feel that pull on the string ... up and down, up and down. It's a toy you don't forget.

Maybe that's because that "Up/Down" rhythm is so characteristic of life. The Stock Market's been very good at it lately. A day's temperature may easily vary 30 or 35 degrees in a 24-hour period. I drop 5 pounds and they yo-yo right back on again if I'm not careful.

There are some ups and downs that I count on. My day ends with the sun going down, and I sleep through the night, confident that I'll awake to the sun's coming up again in the morning. The lows of a cold Winter are forgotten in the highs of a warm Springtime. Some of the events in my life tend to get me down, but I know that as time dissolves the stress, I'll be back up again.

Having faith in the natural ability your body has to recover from the downs is the best anti-depressant medicine there is. So the next time you yo down, be patient with the rhythms of life and know that you'll yo back up again. But don't let go of the string!

# 19.

It's a simple thing to do.... a greeting card at a time when someone needs emotional support. Whether it's expressing sympathy for a loss, or congratulations on a special event in life, it carries with it a message of caring. There is nothing we humans need more.

That caring may be expressed in e-mails, though that feels a little superficial to me. Phone calls have the advantage of a live human voice with the message coming through in the tones of the voice that are as important as the spoken words.

In a past culture, a personal visit to the home of a friend was the norm. There is still nothing as satisfying as a hand or a hug that says, "we're here for you to share this moment with you." It is sad that we do not have as easy access to each other's homes as we had in a more relaxed society.

So greeting cards play an important role in our relationships. Cards have been part of our lives for many years. Hallmark boasts a "card for every occasion," and the card racks expand with the many choices. I confess that I have spent many hours looking for "just the right one."

Part of the fun of card-shopping, however, is that I have met some interesting people doing the same, and in our side-by-side search, we have shared a chuckle over the clever graphics and wording of some of the cards. What an interesting way to form instant, though temporary friendships! It seems that market places, card shops included, encourage us to ignore the fences and reach out to other humans in our common quest.

I think that instinct to be open to each other, to share each other's lives, even in brief encounters, is what makes me say, when there is a special time in a friend's life, "I need to send a card."

# 20.

One of the duties of a minister is to visit with members of the congregation who are in the hospital. I was in my first church, trying to be an effective pastor, so I regularly made the rounds as I was expected to do.

I quickly discovered that those "duties" turn out to be some of the most memorable experiences anyone can have. Mrs. Curtis was in her 80's. Her husband worked across from their home in a fish market. They were a well-matched couple except in one way. He always smelled like fish. She always smelled like fresh baked bread. They were not members you "call on." They were people I dropped in to see frequently because they were so refreshingly wise and unpretending.

I was saddened to learn that Mrs. Curtis would be in the hospital with gangrene on her foot. Part of the leg would have to be removed to save her life. I stood at her bedside trying to find words of comfort. I was just beginning to learn the art of pastoral prayer, and. I was not finding the words. Sensing my nervousness, she said, "Would you like me to pray for you?"

I learned later that the doctor had come in the night before the operation to counsel with her. He had said to her, "Now, Mrs. Curtis, we have a big day tomorrow. You get a good night's sleep."

"Are you the surgeon who will be performing the operation?" she asked. "Yes, I am." he told her.

"Then you go home and get a good night's sleep!" she said.

I learned from a woman who had lived a long time and was now facing a major loss, how faith and courage work together and how ministry works both ways.

# 21.

When I was nearing retirement, a friend, already retired, said to me, "I wake up in the morning with a whole day ahead, but by noon, I'm already two hours behind." He was right; and I fell into the same trap.

I blame myself! I don't have to serve on every committee; I don't have to say "yes" to everything that comes along, even though (or especially because) I'm flattered to be asked. Nor ... and this does frighten me a bit ... do I need to fill up my hours because I wouldn't know what to do with myself if I had some unclaimed time.

I blame my friends, too, for fostering in me, with all good intentions, the feeling that "keeping busy" is a mark of successful retirement.

I am told that the first responsibility of a caregiver is to take care of one's self; else there would be burnout and an end to the ability to provide care for others. Is it not true that we experience an inner hunger if we do not protect time for ourselves, for personal enrichment, for relaxed pacing of life, for personal friendships that are built around the mutual, unconditional give and take of being human together.

I enjoy the feeling of being useful. I enjoy the feeling of being able to provide the lift that someone needs to help them over the hurdles. I enjoy working with others to get a needed job done. But I can't let my life be run by the calendar! I want some space to be spontaneous sometimes, to be free to respond to the moment. I like the kind of innocent 'interaction represented by the 6 year old, who said, following the death of her grandmother, "Grandpa, when you get lonesome for Grandma, you can come and sit with me."

I'm not giving up service projects, but one project must be that of serving myself. There are some good books out there, some good music, some good friends. And I'm not quite ready to give up the child in me. I still want some time just to play.

# 22.

I was fourth in my high school graduating class of 150. That was 3 short of being number one ... Not bad, but not good enough for the top spot of Valedictorian. I wonder sometimes, could I have tried harder early in those 4 years. I don't remember even thinking about graduation when I was a Freshman or Sophomore. By the time I was a Senior, it was too late to sharpen up the years already in the records.

Ben Franklin said, "Never put off...." I'd like to add, never say, "It's good enough." The totals will inevitably be posted. If we don't score in the first inning, the runs won't be included in the final score. If we don't plan for retirement, well ahead of time, the dollars won't be there when we need them.

We like to play with the maxims ... " never do today what you can put off till tomorrow." We laugh at that reversal because it strikes too close to home. In the every day routines of life, we lose the vision of the years we have yet to live, and the zeroes of wasted days are averaged into the final accounting.

Now, let's not get paranoid about this. Rest times are essential for good health if they are built into a comfortable rhythm of living. However, we fall too easily into the trap of one man's comment, "I decided to procrastinate, but I haven't gotten around to it yet." The today I thought I'd have for catching up on yesterday's plans often proves to be tomorrow already.

We're well past High School, but Retirement is still another starting point with every reason to set some new goals and enjoy the fun of working with them every day. Let's not get "old" too fast, by putting off constructing our new life. As a wise Senior put it, "Don't let your wild oats turn into prune juice and all-bran." That's not good enough.

# 23.

Yes, there was the Blacksmith shop we were warned to stay away from ... but, of course, warnings only tell kids that it's a fascinating place to be. So we hung around, enjoying the sparks and the clang of the heavy hammer, and the colorful language of the blacksmith ... until we were shooed away.

And there was the hay mow that we played in, except when the big fork was loading in another cutting. It was fun to dodge that big fork coming in through the upper door in the barn ... until we were chased out. Every one of us was at one time or another buried in the hay. I still sneeze thinking about working my way out from under.

Then, there was the butter to churn ... up and down, up and down until our shoulders ached, each of us taking a turn and none daring to admit that our muscles were crying out for mercy. At least, to ease the pain, there was always that fresh sweet buttermilk as a reward when we were finished.

But of all the memories of growing up on a farm, the one that made the deepest impression on me was the old country store. Situated on a big lot just across the bridge, it had what seemed like a mile-wide front porch, where you could tie up your horse while you stocked up on the goods you needed. That was where I learned about haggling ... more politely known as "bargaining." No one ever paid the posted price. And no one was ever in a hurry. A purchase might take a half an hour of dickering, interspersed with bits of neighborhood gossip. Meanwhile the larger issues of the world were being settled by a half dozen men sitting at the checker board. And while all that was going on, it was easy to reach down into the pickle barrel ... best pickles I've ever tasted! Such a relaxed way of life ... so different from the pressured check-out lines of today!

Next time I go to the supermarket, I think I'll take my checkerboard and set it up by the Service counter and see who joins me. I'll bet it will be the person behind the Service counter.

# 24.

I have been fascinated by shadows from the time when, as children, we played "shadow tag" ... trying to step on each other's shadows while attempting to keep our own out of range. For some primitive cultures, shadows are considered part of one's self; stepping on them is seen as an act of hostility. It's interesting now to look back and see a child's game echoing a primitive superstition.

I early discovered hand shadows and funny animal shapes you could create with your fingers. I grew up with the flickering lights of candles and oil lamps and knew the wonderful story-land you could create if you let your imagination play with the mysteries of dancing shadows in a semi-lit room.

I enjoy the morning sun when I can watch the advancing shadows move slowly across the frosty grass, and watch the pictures appear on the walls and ceiling from the sun catchers on the windows. The variety of shadow patterns is endless ... sometimes lacy designs as the sun filters through the leaves, sometimes sharp silhouettes of objects standing against the sun. Our ancestors marked the passing of time with shadows ... a stick set in the ground, and later the sundial.

Robert Louis Stevenson wrote for children, "I have a little shadow that goes in and out with me, and what can be the use of him is more than I can see."

I can't help noting that even as I write, it is with two pens, the one I hold in my hand and the shadow pen that always rises to meet the pen point at the paper. Shadows are an integral part of our language. The Psalms: (17) "Hide me in the shadow of thy wings." and (102) "My days are like an evening shadow." We speak of "shadowing" if we are following someone. We stand in the "shadow" of great leaders. And some wag has written, "When small men cast long shadows, it is a sign of the setting sun."

I find it so interesting that the most intimate presence in our lives is, in fact, a presence actually created by an absence ... the interruption of light. Having no depth, my shadow is yet an inescapable extension of myself. I hate to think what it would be like not to have a shadow.

photo by Paul Barfoot

# 25.

It was a stupid thing to do, setting a ladder in the mud, in the rain, trying to clean out an overflowing gutter! That's how I broke my hand, an unsafe ladder and off to the emergency room.

But like many careless things we do, there was a learning in it. I'm right handed. I discovered while my hand was in a cast how badly I had neglected the training of my left hand. It took some determined practice even to write my name. I became keenly conscious of the benefit of having, not just two hands, but two opposing hands. Imagine lifting a heavy bag of groceries with two right hands, or picking up a child with two left hands.

I thought about opposites in life. Rainy days and sunny days, for example. Opposites? Yes, but more accurately, complementary to each other, for we need both and are in trouble if we have only one without the other.

Consider sound and silence. What a relief sometimes to hit the mute button on the remote! Or on the other hand (so to speak) to hear the phone ring, with a friendly voice on the other end, when the silence of a lonely day becomes oppressive. Jack Benny had a way of using timely pauses that brought out dramatically the comic impact of his routines. The rests in a musical score are essential to the fullness of the melody.

Is it not so also with joy and sorrow? Opposites, yes. Yet both are integral parts of emotional health. If we never experience pain, we shall never really enjoy vigorous health. If life is all ease and comfort, how shall we train ourselves in the disciplines of courage and inner strength for the times of crisis?

I look at my folded hands and thank God for the opposites in life that come together in interlocking wholeness.

# 26.

    His eyes were full of adventure. In his hand was a stick that he had just picked up. A casual observer would see a broken piece of tree limb. To a little boy, it was much more.... it was anything his imagination might create. A magic wand, an instrument for rat-a-tat on picket fences, something to poke into ant hills.

    You could toss stones into the air and swing at them. You could play "fetch" with your dog. You could draw pictures in the dirt. A "flag" tied to it would take you sailing off on a pirate ship or into space on a rocket. Only the imagination would limit the things a stick could be and do. A stick was security, something a boy could grasp with his hand, something he owned and didn't have to put away neatly with his other toys. It had the feel of being a companion. No offering from the toy store could have as much versatility.

    A stick is good for a boy to have, better even than a Nintendo. No instructions come with a stick. It's not programmed by someone else; a boy can program it according to his own fantasies and only he has the password to its possibilities.

    Someday in later years, the boy may carry another stick. Let's not call it a "cane" that emphasizes dependency, but a walking stick that still invites imagination. It may be made of a special wood, like hickory, perhaps carved or decorated to add story to it, or handed down by his grandfather, or brought over from the old country with its own story.

    A boy needs a stick to open up a world of adventures. And when the years catch up with him, hopefully, there will be enough of the young boy left in the old man to let his imagination still open up some fantasies with his walking stick, making it a prop, as in a drama, not just as in a handicap!

# 27.

You can always get my attention by dropping a coin or speaking my name. A coin is simply an instrument of commerce, a token for trading—value for value. A name, however, is a symbolic contract between society and an individual. It is a passport to the essential services the society offers its members.

A name may reflect a sense of ancestry, as "Donaldson," or it may be a means of honoring a friend or relative in naming a newborn child. In some cultures, names are chosen by incantation and have an aura of magic for a lifetime. A given name, in fact, may be only the first of several names given throughout life in recognition of milestones in that life. Without names, it would be impossible to record the history of a society.

Every great faith finds its focus in the name of God. In the Jewish faith, the name carries such power that it is spoken or written only in symbolic form. Islam worships Allah and each section of its scriptures begins "In the name of God...". The story of Christmas is the story of a birth and a naming. The angel's instruction to Joseph: "Take Mary as your wife ... she will have a son and you shall name him Jesus." As the Christian faith developed, "Christ" was added. That name has become an essential part of the name of the celebration of his birth even though the season of Christmas has become saturated with secular commercialism. The **name** reminds us of the **nature** of the day.

To speak my name derisively is to injure my identity. I may never recover from the effects of gossip and slander. It is not surprising that the very First Commandment warns against the abusive use of the name of the Lord, but this has implications for humans too. By the way we use a name, we may value or de-value the one who bears it. Friend, speak my name gently, I pray; its value may be in your hands!

# 28.

Faith always comes wrapped in a story. Simply to "believe" without the supporting narrative, is like trying to sing a song without the music. The Christian concept of redemption would be merely a religious theory without the stories of the angels and the shepherds, of a supper in an upstairs room and an empty tomb after a crucifixion. The stories of Abraham and Moses and the Passover are critical to the Jewish understanding of themselves as a chosen people.

I believe in love, but it would take a story, not a definition, to communicate what love is. The words alone are sterile. I need to tell you about a relationship between two people that is fulfilling to both, and you will understand by living in that story with them. I need to tell you of the man who ran barefoot across a wide stretch of sharp stones to rescue a drowning boy from the river. I need to tell you of a mother who held her asthmatic child in her arms all night to comfort and calm her.

We live by stories. We tell our friends of the trip we took. But don't give me just the physical dimensions of that great Cathedral you saw. Show me the pictures, yes, but tell me the story of your entrance into it and how you interacted with what you saw, and how you felt. Take me with you; let me feel it with you. I may forget the pictures, but I'll remember your stories. If you asked me to describe my grandfather, it would be useless for me to tell you of his physical features. You would not see him as I saw him until I tell you of the experiences we shared, the stories he told.

The great religions all have their scriptures, filled with admonitions and values by which to live. But they are not lectures. They are tales to inform, to inspire, to interpret what those values are through living experiences. The Truth is embedded in the story. And it is not forgotten, because the story relates to our own experiences; the story becomes our own story and the Truth becomes our own Faith.

# 29.

I was fired from my first job. I was 10 years old. There was a small neighborhood A&P store down the street where all the customers were know by name and Mr. Munro, the storekeeper, was known for his warm personal service.

One day, he said to me, "How would you like to bag potatoes for me? I'll give you a penny a bag." That was wealth! I could probably do 15 to 20 bags at a time, a couple times a week. I was suddenly rich. I spent a whole morning carefully weighing out the correct number of pounds for each bag. "A peck of potatoes," I kept repeating to myself, "a peck of potatoes." It had such a musical sound ... like money!

The next day I came in and headed for the potato bin. Mr. Munro interrupted me. "I can't let you do this any more", he said, "A lady complained that her peck was short a pound. I can't afford to sell potatoes that aren't full weight." I went away crushed. I had done what I thought was a competent job. I quickly learned the art of blaming others: "The scales were off." "The customer was scheming to get an extra pound of potatoes." "Mr. Munro had changed his mind about the penny deal and was using this as an easy out."

These days, there are convenient scales in grocery stores where you can check the accuracy of the weight marked on the package. I seldom see anyone doing that, however. Today, customers don't seem to question the weight, they just gasp at the price.

I wish I could find the lady who complained about my potatoes. I have enough pennies now that I could buy her an extra pound of potatoes to put in her peck. I'd like to have my job back, not for the pennies, but to redeem my reputation. But then second chances don't always depend on potatoes, and I've never been fired from a job since.

# 30.

In a world of crowded schedules and the frenzied pursuit of the advantages of life, I find myself turning back to those relaxed summer evenings on the porch. The supper dishes finished, the dog fed, and the routine end-of-the-day chores taken care of, we had about an hour of sundown time just to settle ourselves down before we lit the lamps and began to get ready for bed.

There was a softness about the twilight that was a tonic for tired muscles. The wisps of smoke from my grandpa's evening pipe drifted slowly upward to dissolve in the gathering shadows about us. The cool quiet was healing, the conversation pleasant. A few words here and there seemed like simple lyrics in tune with the rhythm of the rocking chairs.

The cricket songs, the tiny flashes of fireflies, and the moon on its way across the sky, outlining the tree tops against a graying canvas, combined to add a touch of mystery and beauty that had a calming effect. It was as though the concerns of the day had been dissipated in an expanded space that now allowed for dreamy fantasies and deep breathing.

If I have one resolution for the New Year, it is to remind myself to take time for those moments of renewal. I don't have a porch today, but I have its memories and the sense of peace that comes with the remembering of those relaxed twilight times when the fading light seemed to take the tensions of the day with it. And I know that my body and mind demand a regular bathing in the magic of something like that "summer porch" time, even for brief moments, if they are to stay healthy.

# 31.

The speaker had presented his subject clearly and with an enthusiasm that made for easy listening. As he concluded, he said, "Are there any questions?" There was dead silence. He asked again, "No questions?" The audience shifted uncomfortably but no one spoke a word. After an awkward hesitation, he sat down, clearly disappointed. Had all that he had said stimulated no further interest in his listeners? He would never know.

A question may be asking only for specific information. I ask you, "What is your name?" and you give me an exact answer. But if I ask you, "Where does your name come from?" that opens up a world of history and heritage. I get a fascinating story, and a happy relationship with another human being.

Children are instinctively questioners. "Why?" is an early part of their vocabulary. Curiosity is the engine for their learning. Touching is their connection with the things-to-be-discovered that come new to them every day. Wonder is the key that opens up things-to-be-explored.

How important it is to carry over into our older years, that sense of adventure, the eagerness to learn what makes things work, how things came to be, why things (and people) act the way they do. The chances are we'll never know unless we ask. Learning to ask questions may well be the most important skill we must develop in order to participate fully in the world in which we live. We meet a friend and ask, "How are you?" ... not so much to inquire about a state of health as to open up a conversation. We learn as we listen, with one question triggering another and building growing relationships and understandings and archives of information in our heads that stimulate even more questions.

It's hard to imagine a world in which there would be no more questions to ask, no more discoveries to make, no more sense of wonder, all information neatly wrapped up! Even so, there would be one more question: "Where do we go from here ... what happens next?"

# 32.

We sometimes refer, poetically, to the passing of the years as the "Summer of Life" or the "Winter of Life." Somewhere in between must be the "Fall of Life," those years when we're not young any more, but we certainly aren't old.

With an increasing life expectancy, there is a challenge to spending as many as 20 or 30 years beyond retirement in creative and satisfying ways. Some of us continue working past the magic 65 number; some of us find that volunteering opens up all kinds of new experiences and friendships. Some of us keep busy almost as a defense against having to discover new avenues that give life new meaning.

It takes some courage and flexibility to walk new paths that lead us to places with which we are not familiar. We don't like to be the strangers in the crowd. We joke about our resistance to change ... "We've never done it that way before," or when change comes to our neighborhood, we say, "Not in my back yard."

Yet, the happiest people I know are those who have ventured out into new areas and discovered that they have talents they have never called on. One man I know has made a retirement career out of making hooked rugs. Another has become an expert at quilting and now is teaching others this craft. The rush to learn computing is amazing. Chair caning is a very popular class at Senior Centers. Dance clubs are thriving as we discover that those legs move more easily in response to music. The Advancing years can certainly be The Fulfilling years.

Even in the natural world, some of the most beautiful flowers bloom in September. Trees are at the height of their color in October. November is full of the warmth of the spirit if not of the weather. And December is Celebration Time, filled with joy and song. If the Seasons refused to change, all of that would be lost.

Is it not also so, with humans?

# 33.

The other day, I took the bus into town. I dropped into a seat and closed my eyes. I'd seen the scenery along the way many times. This was a good time to catch a few winks.

But if I was expecting a dull 20-minute ride, the whole scene changed at the next stop. A four-year-old got on with his Mom and suddenly the bus came alive. Up and down the aisle, trying every empty seat, he screamed with delight in his excitement with a ride on a bus. His face pressed against the window, seeing things I had never noticed before.

I wondered where I had lost the sense of adventure. My mind turned back to my first ride in my Uncle's Model T. I felt a flicker of nostalgia as I remembered the open streetcars that we used to ride to the Fair. In those days of innocence a trip in any public conveyance meant "going somewhere," an excursion, with a destination that held bright promise of something out of the ordinary.

I glanced at the other passengers around me. Blank stares told me of the effect of routine. It was if they had opted out of the world for this short bus ride. If they noticed the little boy, it was with annoyance that he had interrupted their mindless boredom.

I decided to get off a stop early and walk a couple blocks through a neighborhood I had not seen before. I found it exciting to notice what people had done to make their yards neat and attractive. I found the variety of front doors made a kind of area mosaic. I spoke to a man sitting on his porch and had a moment of friendly conversation. There were children playing, and I lingered to enjoy their laughter. A squirrel on a branch above my head caught my eye, and I stopped to marvel about life in all its forms.

I think I was late for wherever I was going that day, but I didn't apologize to anyone. How could I have explained that a little boy's bursting energy had opened my eyes, on the bus, and for the rest of the day.

# 34.

For the first time in my life, I walked past a penny lying on the ground. I mean, I actually ignored it, even though I saw it quite clearly there in front of me. I rationalized that I had my hands full and it wasn't worth the risk of dropping something I was carrying.

It wasn't a big thing, and yet, there was Ben Franklin standing beside me with his famous, "A penny saved …." and there was my thrifty father reminding me, that "Every penny counts." I recalled the e-mail someone had sent me: "You know you're old when nothing less than a quarter is worth bending over to pick up." Was I really that old?

I thought of my old penny bank and the satisfaction of the jingle of the coins inside. I remembered the penny candy store and how wealthy I felt when I once had four pennies in my hand and filled a small candy bag. I found myself humming the little ditty we sang as we dropped our birthday pennies into the Sunday School jar.

I smiled as I heard again the excited voices of my friends, laying pennies on the railroad track to be smashed by the train wheels. I kept the two that were mine for years as tokens of … I'm not sure … my boyhood I guess. I had just received some pennies in change at the store and for just an adventurous moment, I wondered where I might find the nearest train tracks.

I put the groceries in the car and stood there reflecting on how important pennies had been in life. I retraced my steps and, to the amusement of the man whom I had to ask to move his foot, picked up the penny and put in my pocket.

# 35.

I'm not a big sports fan. I can watch a team win or lose if the game is played well. It's the skills of the players of the game that I enjoy. I like to follow those who stand out for consistent performance, the ones whose names go down in the record books and in the hearts of the fans. We love our heroes, the ones for whom we can cheer. We mentally suit up with our favorites and ingest a piece of their accomplishments for ourselves.

If our loyalty is genuine, it will not disappear when our aging heroes are no longer able to run the bases. They will be remembered as persons who gave credit to the game on the field and genuine entertainment to the spectators who played the game from their seats.

We need heroes. Through those whom we admire, we broaden our life experience. They carry our imaginations beyond our own ability or experience. They open horizons for us that are a step above where we live. We swing the bat with them and ride the ball into the stands.

Happily, it happens to all of us, young and old. We lived in Boston for a couple years. One day, my father said, "How would you like to see a real ball game?" Off we went to the stadium with its smell of popcorn and hot dogs and the boisterous noise of a cheering crowd. Caught up in my baseball-loving Father's excitement, I watched a big man step to the plate. I was only 6 at the time and hardly realized the significance of what I was watching, but I eagerly joined in the cheering.

I don't know who won the game, but the memory has been a joy all my life, the day that Babe Ruth and I hit a home run.

# 36.

I'm a "clipper".... noteworthy news items, amusing cartoons, insightful editorials, inspiring verse, announcements involving people I know, especially if there are pictures.

The pages of my grandmother's Bible were interleafed with things she had saved. I find my clippings in odd places.... in a book I've been reading, in the pile on my desk, in a pocket I haven't worn recently. Mostly, I have a drawer in which I preserve these treasures for future information, or inspiration.

To tell the truth, I couldn't say what's in the drawer.... some outdated information, pictures of people I have forgotten, obsolete advice on Mutual Funds, perhaps, all saved for later reviewing. The drawer is getting pretty full. I must weed it out to make room for the more current clippings! In a way, clippings are like flowers, attractive when fresh, but losing their appeal after a few days. You can discard flowers, but not clippings. Even though I may not remember why I cut them out in the first place, they are a collection of things I have found interesting through the years.

Clipping can be a compelling habit. I'm usually eating breakfast when I see something I want to cut out.... as soon as I finish reading the paper. Then a couple days later, I remember it and go searching through the yesterdays' papers. Sometimes, as if by some sorcery, all the pages are there, except the one I'm searching for; or the item I had seen hides from me until I have combed through the pages again and again to find it.

I once missed the fourth in a series of six articles. I knew that everyone on my block took the same paper, so I went rummaging through a dozen neighbors' recycle bins before I found it. I don't recommend this practice. People stare at you!

But there they lie, my clippings that have seemed so critical to save, gathering dust in the drawer. Someday, when I have time to look at them again, I wonder what I'll find!

# 37.

What I miss most in retirement is routine. I used to get up with the alarm, get ready and off to work with never a thought. I knew how long it took to shave, to grab a quick breakfast, how many minutes to the office ... and how long it took for me to get my mind working when I got to my desk.

Now I have to decide whether to get out of bed or ignore the alarm. (There are sometimes some internal pressures that make that decision for me.) I have to decide whether to shave before or after breakfast. I even have time to think what kind of cereal I want this time.

All this requires thinking. I have run on habit for so many years! Now I have to pay attention to which key I put in the ignition. I reach an intersection and have to think, "Am I turning right to the store, or left to the library?"

Dinner was always when I got home from work. Coffee breaks and lunch times were predetermined by office schedules. Now I not only have to think what I'm going to do each day, but, when I'm busy with it, consciously interrupt for meal time. I have to check the clock and think, "It's noon; that's lunch time."

So much trouble to have to think! I used to put on my shoes in the dark. Now I have to look closely to see which is the left and which is the right, and if the socks are the same color. Even setting my pill bottles lined up in front of me, I have to think, "Did I take the one in the green bottle yet?" It seems the older I get, the more things I have to think about, things to decide, things to remember.

I wonder if I could retrain my brain with a new set of routines that would put me back on automatic again and save me the hassle of having to think.

I'll think about it.

# 38.

I no longer put things I may frequently need on the top shelf. My shoulders have learned too well the language of "ouch" when I reach too high. It's like shifting gears. I stretch part way and stop. Then, with some persuasion, my hand reaches the rest of the way if I stand on tiptoe; or even better if I can find a stool that gives me a little height advantage.

But shelves have depth as well as height, and finding what I'm reaching for takes a bit of exploration. My fingers can distinguish bottles from packages, but can't read labels, so I have to take down (or knock down) several items before I find what I am looking for. The other day, I decided to take a drastic step. I took everything off that shelf and cleaned it as best I could. I even threw out a few little bottles that looked like they had been there forever.

This is where I began to strategize. There's that ugly blue dish that cousin Sally gave us last Christmas. Top shelf! What a neat hiding place! I hate dill pickles ... good place for them! There's the salt shaker. If I put it out of sight, I won't be tempted to compromise my salt-free diet. So I went through the items that could be made innocently inaccessible, and one by one pushed them to the rear of the top shelf.

Satisfied that I might never need to reach that high again, I made room on the lower shelves for the items that remained ... I didn't even make a list of the things that went back up there ... I just abandoned them. "How wise I am", I told myself, "If I'm going to have aging joints, I can at least find creative ways of protecting them."

The next day, I heard my wife unusually busy in the kitchen. I came out to see what she was doing. Everything I had put up on that pesky shelf was now sitting on the kitchen counter. "What in the world ... " I said. She turned, "Have you seen my new medicine? I put it up here on the top shelf where it wouldn't get lost."

# 39.

How did we ever allow the fork to dictate the rules of social dining? I'm putting in my bid for the return of the spoon as an eating instrument as graceful as the fork ... and more practical.

I wouldn't think of trying to eat my soup or stir my coffee with a fork. And for rounding up those elusive little peas, a fork is of little use unless you have something like mashed potatoes on your plate to mix with them.

A piece of cake inevitably falls off both sides of my fork. I try to stab a ripe olive or a cherry tomato, only to watch it go skidding off into someone's lap ... Tomatoes can squirt irresponsibly unless they are treated with respect. Rather than stabbing them with a fork, how much easier to roll them into the bowl of a spoon, and stay in command. (The side of a fork does make a nice "pusher" for getting things onto your spoon.)

Sadly, we first teach children how to use a spoon. And as soon as they've accomplished that, we lay a fork by their plate and tell them it's not grown-up to use a spoon. A fork is helpful to hold my meat steady while I cut it, but, after all, forks are only a poor imitation of fingers. With fingers, I can surround what I'm picking up and bring it safely to my mouth. How else do you eat a chicken leg, for example?

Many meals use gravy to moisten and add flavor to the meat and potato. I'm always sorry that much of the flavor is left on the plate when I have finished my meal, but I'm told that it's not polite to tip my plate and scoop up the remaining juice with a spoon!

Oh well, I still have a piece of bread in my hand. At least I can sop up the good flavor with that.

# 40.

Sometimes I think, "There ought to be a law!" As one Senior said to me: "The most depressing part of the day is the news." Yet, we are lost without the daily newspaper. We are glued to the TV for the evening news. We have a modern day mania for keeping in touch with events of the day as reported by a variety of newscasters. We seem spellbound by the grim side of the news.

There seems to be plenty of tragic news to fill several pages of the newspaper every day, but suppose it were required that half the reports would be news that would make us feel happy instead of gloomy. Suppose reporters were assigned to the stories of human kindness as well the sensational and that those stories were given equal space.

Those stories often happen spontaneously and simply, so they are gone before they can get a reporter to cover them. So, maybe it's up to us to be the reporters as we share the good things that happen to us.

For example, I had carried from the store to my car, a couple heavy bags of groceries. As I set them down to open the trunk, a twelve-year-old boy came up and said, "Are you finished shopping?" Before I could answer, he had lifted the bags into the trunk and skipped off to help someone else down the line. I stood uncertain for a moment, it had happened so quickly. He disappeared before I could say "thank you," but I felt the fun he was having in simply helping people, and I felt lifted myself by his buoyant spirit.

It all took place in less than a minute, but I have had many minutes of joy sharing the story of that carefree act of kindness. Once in a while such a story does get into the newspapers, and I rejoice.

No, there shouldn't be a law! We don't need a law; we need, ourselves, to be the reporters who, every day, have the joy of telling each other the stories that lift our spirits and brighten our day.

# 41.

We always said Grace at mealtimes in our family. As a child, I accepted the custom, though I had no idea what the word "Grace" meant. It was something you said before you could start eating. I understood that it was a prayer, but it didn't help that I had an Aunt Grace, whom I didn't like very well. And I wondered why her name should be attached to a prayer. I would have gladly called the prayer "Joan" or Betty" or even by my mother's name "Laura". I wondered why my father hadn't thought of that. After all, it was she who prepared and served our meals.

It wasn't until I was married and we had our own chldren that I began to see Grace as more than a few words zipped through before the food got cold. It seemed like everybody came to the supper table rushed. The kids had been out playing and had to hurry to wash their hands. I was constantly busy with the never-ending responsibilities of a pastor and was emotionally drained by late afternoon ... And, of course, there was the stressful task in the kitchen of getting everything ready to set on the table at the same time ... and calling everyone to be at the table at the same time.

We surely wanted to say thanks for the food that was on our table. But Grace became more than that. It was like taking a deep breath and letting all the racing inside us quiet down. We had all been off on our own all day, but we always held hands during grace and in just that minute or two, we came together to enjoy our supper. We were family again.

I have found many uses for Grace other than at mealtimes.

Many times, in my life, just a minute or two of pausing with a "Grace" to pull myself together when I feel I'm coming apart ... puts me back on track again.

# 42.

Time moves swiftly, and you can't go back. But you can think back. A group of us old folks were talking about things in our past that will never be again, and what we miss most. Martha, a 93 year old, with her hands gesturing to match the words, spoke up. "I miss carrying wood and pumping water." she said.

We'd been talking about kerosene lamps, and hard beds and washtubs and such. No one had said they missed these ... just remembered them. Martha took me in a new direction. I remembered, as a boy, the satisfaction of filling the wood bin in the kitchen, ready for Grandma when she was baking.

I remembered priming that old long-handled pump, coaxing it to fill my pail with that fresh, cool water from the well. I remembered my Grandpa's stern instruction ... "Don't drink it all; leave some for the next prime." I enjoyed learning to accomplish things with my own hands. He added the important "planning ahead" part.

I used to repair my own tires, crank the engine and cheer when it started, I am grateful for the mechanical and technological improvements that we have seen in our lifetime. But now with everything automated, I am aware that I am not as sharp with some of the manual and mental skills I once depended on.

There's a need for some places in life where I find pleasure in doing-it-myself ... feeling my muscles flex, my brain stretching. At least I still enjoy totalling up my bill in my head sometimes, before the cashier has entered everything in the computer, and surprising her by having ready the exact amount.

# 43.

I'm like Charlie Brown. I always reach into my mailbox with anticipation. Who knows, maybe someday there'll be a letter from Barbra Streisand inviting me to do a show with her. I wade through bills and catalogues, requests for money and announcements of events that I "mustn't miss." I marvel at the seductive writing of the ads and try to imagine who writes them and addresses me, personally, as "Dear Earl." The next day I'm there again, eager to see what treasure is in the mail today. It costs me nothing to fantasize and it makes junk mail a lot more fun.

One day, I really had a surprise. I had recently written a check and mailed it to pay an insurance bill. A couple weeks later, I had a call from the office secretary, asking if I would like to bring in the other half of the check. I recognized the smile in her voice, so I went over to the office, wondering what kind of joke this was.

She handed me an envelope from the Rochester Post Office. I opened it and several scraps of paper fell out on the table. Sure enough, they pieced together as half of the check. The Post Office had included a note of apology. Fortunately, a piece of the envelope on which I had written the Insurance Company's address had been recovered, so the pieces of the check had been forwarded to the Insurance office. One piece of the check had my name on it, so the office had been able to identify me as the sender.

I figured the Insurance agent had half his money so I offered to write a new check for the other half, but he didn't buy it. I wrote a new check for the full amount and took home my letter from the Post Office. Two days later, in my own mailbox, was another letter from Rochester with the rest of the pieces of the check, and another letter of apology.

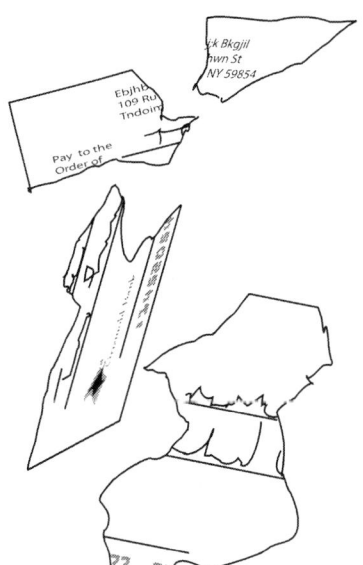

I keep those pieces as a symbol of the personal care the Post Office gives us. What other business will go out of its way to find you and show you how efficiently they have shredded your checks and even apologize in case you weren't satisfied? But, you know, I think the next time the Insurance Company raises my premium, I'll tear up the check myself.

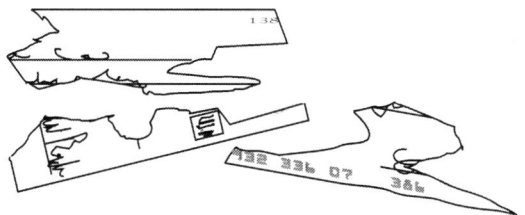

# 44.

Have you ever had your brain taken over by a song that runs through your head all day long? From somewhere in the back of your memory, the tune pops up and won't let go. You have no idea why this particular song claimed your attention at this time. Some sound or smell or color or circumstance is a trigger, and you realize that the song is forever attached to some experience you have had long ago. It is not forgotten ... just lying there in a far corner of your mind until it is called up from the past by an association with something in the now.

For some unknown reason, I found myself humming an old college song the other day ... a song I haven't thought of in 65 years! At first, I could only recall a few words, but as the tune ran round and round in my head, it began picking up the words, random at first, but gradually whole phrases, until I had reclaimed the whole song, I was amazed at how, as the tune and the words came together, I was on campus again, seeing faces of old friends, feeling the musty smell of old Baker Hall, hearing the big bell calling us to Chapel.

My favorite game, when I'm behind the wheel for an extended drive, is to recall old songs, one at a time. I begin with an "A" song like "Always" and run on through the alphabet, enjoying the memories each song calls up. Sometimes I can reach back and pull up the words. Sometimes, I don't know the words and enjoy just humming the tune.

But, why wait until I'm behind the wheel! Anytime I'm behind, I can pick up my spirits by letting my Music Memory Bank take over. If you hear me singing to myself, it's just that I've put myself on automatic. It's a great anti-depression strategy.

# 45.

Of all the things I have heard said, following the World Trade Center disaster, the phrase that I shall not forget is, "America has lost its innocence."

In spite of crime and corruption and greed, from which our country is surely not exempt, the American people have been a trusting society. The vegetable stand where I buy our summer produce is a good example. Driver after driver pulls up, selects purchases and with no attendant in sight, deposits money in a box marked "self-service." That the owners continue to do this is evidence that the honor system has worked.

In the wake of the terrorist attacks on America, we may never feel quite as secure again, but what a lonely world it would be if we should lose that sense of trusting each other. How terrible if our anger, for lack of a better target, should be vented on those close to us, or if our fear should keep us from mingling with the communities that are the very centers of our lives.

Several years ago, I was held up in a street robbery. Today, I am not afraid to walk on the street, but I am keenly aware of shadows, of footsteps behind me, of surroundings that are not friendly. We know that we are vulnerable, personally and nationally, that evil is a reality, and to be ever on the alert is a necessity. But this is not a reason to run and hide in fear, nor to bury ourselves in anxiety. It is all the more reason to strengthen the ties of family and of friends and experience that trust and love which is our only security.

Lost our innocence? Rather, we have found our need to come together to care for each other. Our deepest sympathy goes to those who lost their lives and loved ones in the atrocious attack on September 11th. But how significant that every one of the messages from the doomed planes or buildings included the words, "I love you!"

Let those words be enshrined as their legacy to America. Let us not lose that treasure even in the midst of our shock and grief.

# 46.

    I sometimes wonder why I am willing to undertake a task, knowing there will be hours of work ahead before it is completed. In college, we were given an outline of responsibilities for the whole semester's course. At first glance, it was staggering, but by dividing it into smaller sections, I found it was achievable. Through many similar experiences, I have learned that there is nothing as gratifying as looking at an achievement and being glad that you were willing to do the work it needed along the way.

    It's like that with Christmas shopping. I look at the list of people who are "must" for gifts. Then I begin to toss in a few names for whom a simple gift would be a nice recognition of a special friendship or of a special service someone has done for me. The list grows, and I realize that shopping for "just the right gift" for each one would be too tedious. A personal note for many on the list takes less time and is actually a more effective personal remembrance ... and more fun.

    For some, I pick a small something that would sit attractively on their coffee table. For the "musts," I first turn the "obligation" into an "adventure." My shopping list in hand, I cruise the stores until something pops out at me. "Jean would like that" ... "That would fit in with Dave's hobby" ... "My wife has always wanted one of those."

    The price I must pay is not only the dollars, however, but the planning ahead for the hours this takes. If I begin early and see this as an adventure and don't try to do it all at once, it becomes a series of achievements and, in essence, I've also had the pleasure of taking my friends and family along with me.

# 47.

I do crossword puzzles for relaxation. If I can't fill in all the spaces, I don't worry about it. Tomorrow's paper will reveal the ones I missed. It's a brain game and fun to figure out some of the clever definitions.

Sometimes, I come back to the puzzle I left unfinished yesterday, without looking at today's paper. I'm always surprised that some of the words that had stumped me when I left it, now become apparent the second time around.

I don't know whether my brain works sometimes and sometimes not, or whether it runs out of speed and I have to prime it again the next day. Or is it that I didn't really put away the puzzle and my brain went on working for the answers, all by itself, and had them ready when I picked up the puzzle again. Or maybe the brain doesn't like to be pushed and says, "Don't force me; let me give you the answer at my own pace." Maybe when I try too hard to think, I just crowd everything together and nothing comes clear.

It's that way when I forget a name. I get embarrassed that I can't remember what I should never have forgotten, and suddenly, later, it pops into my head like it was always there.

I've learned when I misplace something, not to panic in my search for it ... but just to say to my brain, "You know where it is, let me know in your own good time."

Sometimes, I hear someone say, "use your brain," like "turn it up a notch." We do have to plug it in again in those times when we have disconnected, but it's not a high speed computer. I think I'll be happier if I trust it to work OK and not blank it out with anxiety when it chooses to function in a more relaxed mood.

# 48.

Other than Ministers and golfers, I think Doctors must be prime targets for the most jokes. From the favorite quote, "Take an aspirin and call me tomorrow" to the more subtle report to the patient, "I'm afraid we'll have to do a second operation, I can't find my wrist watch," the mysterious world of medical practice lends itself all too easily to humorous digs.

Since I was named after the doctor whose skilled hands brought me into the world, I feel a bit of loyalty to the profession. I know the hours Teachers spend grading papers for their students. I can only guess how much time Doctors spend filling out forms for their patients. I know how easily typos creep into a letter I'm writing; but there can be no margin of error in medicine. A Doctor must be constantly on high alert. One little mistake could be serious. When I had my right knee replaced, I thought it was funny, but I really appreciated the precaution when the surgeon marked in big letters, "THIS ONE" on my right knee.

I watch the TV "pill ads" and I try to picture what it would be like, if everyone "asked their doctor" about all the medicines advertised. Can you imagine taking a list of 15 or 20 medicines you think might apply to your condition and asking the Doctor to run through them with you? True, a patient is responsible for seeking the information needed for treatment, but I'm a little sensitive about pushing a Doctor's patience.

I'm sensitive too about asking for free advice when I see my Doctor in "Civvies." It's only fair that I plan an office visit when I have a concern; and anyway, in most Doctor's waiting rooms, I can enjoy magazines dating all the way back to my boyhood.

# 49.

I seem to be dropping things lately, more than normally.

A spoon that I thought I had in hand ... on the floor! A magazine that slides off my lap. They're pretty slick, but do I have to hold them with both hands? It troubles me that I can't hang on to anything any more. For one thing, it's a little harder to reach down and pick things up ... and even harder, when a pencil or a coin seems determined to roll into the farthest corner of the room, and usually under something. If I could have a maid, her first job would be to pick up the scraps of paper that appear on the floor from nowhere.

I know that my fingers aren't as flexible as they used to be, and my depth perception doesn't always send clear signals to my hands. I find myself setting things down just short of where they should be. I have to be very intentional about where I set my cup of coffee ... I'm constantly having to pick up my comb or tooth brush that I thought I had laid safely on the sink.

My worst problem is the soap in the shower. I've learned to start off with 4 bars in the soap dish so that I can drop as many as 3 and still have one to use.

Is it that my body knows I need the exercise? I'm certainly getting my share of knee-bending these days. My Grandma used to talk about having "Dropsy." I never knew what that was, but maybe I'll adopt that term to describe my difficulty and write it off as a disease.

At least, it will keep me from having to admit that I'm just getting careless in my old age.

# 50.

A group of us were talking about how we would like our grand-children to remember us. One woman said, "I'd like my grand-children to remember that Grandma had a soft lap." I could imagine the comfort and security that a child might feel snuggling down, held close in those loving arms. That was a nice picture.

Another said, "I hope my grand-children will remember that there were always cookies in the cookie jar." I really vibrated with that. When I think of my own grandma, I catch again the wonderful aroma of molasses cookies. She made them often and she made them big ... plate size. She'd say, "You can only have one cookie at a time." and she'd wink, knowing that her size cookies would last us all morning and we wouldn't need a second one ... at least not right away.

What fascinated me, too, was the way she could feed wood into the stove, adjust the dampers, and keep her oven just the right temperature so the cookies never burned. I could help by bringing in wood from the woodpile outside, but she alone controlled the amount and the timing of wood to be added in that old stove. Today's most efficient thermostat couldn't have done better.

And, In a strange way, there was a feeling of contentment when, after the supper dishes were washed, I helped her set the table with the plates and cups turned over and a cloth spread over the dishes, ready for breakfast the next morning.

As a farmer's wife, she was capable and loving. The table always ready for the next meal, an endless supply of big molasses cookies ... and an abundance of hugs. That's how I remember Grandma.

# 51.

     This is the time of year when I get out my old coat and check it out. If I'm wearing a suit, a coat is surely the appropriate thing to wear in cold weather. But as I grow older I am less likely to suit up. I will usually leave the coat where it is and reach for a sweater instead. A coat is heavy on my shoulders, and bulky. It's hard to sit down with it on and often I have to hunt for a place to hang it up. A sweater hugs me and fits my body. It moves comfortably with my arms so that I hardly know I have it on. A coat keeps the cold out, but a sweater keeps the warm in.

     Sweaters come into their own, in what we call the Holiday Season. We not only decorate our homes for the holidays, we can decorate ourselves with the clothes we wear. Sweaters lend themselves to creative possibilities. We can spell out our greetings on them; we can bedeck them with images of Christmas trees and candles and reindeer and all the other symbols of the season. As an ordinary sweater keeps the body warm, the colorful sweaters we wear this time of year seem to keep our spirits aglow.

     It's an interesting paradox that when the winter season brings the longest periods of darkness, we are able to turn on the spirit of love and good will to make it the happiest, brightest time of the year. We find a new lightness and freedom. The joy that is growing inside puts a jubilance in our step and a light in our eyes that almost demands to be shown on the outside in the very clothes we wear. So I think I'll put my coat back on the hanger for now and get out my holiday sweaters,

     'Tis the season!

# 52.

A store owner I once knew used to put the Valentine decorations on the walls, with Christmas displays hung over them, Thanksgiving in front of those, and Hallowe'en trimmings over the whole thing. That was efficiency! At least he focused on one holiday at a time. Thanksgiving waited until Hallowe'en came down. Valentines didn't show until the Santas were put away.

The other day I went into a large department store. There were signs everywhere. Facing me, "Win a Turkey for Thanksgiving". On my right, "Complete selection of Hallowe'en costumes." To my left, "Christmas cards 50% off, in the Trim-a-Tree department." In the clothing department, signs were being readied for a "Winter Coat Clearance Sale."

You could go from one season to another without leaving the store. I couldn't decide whether to buy of bag of candy corn or jump the season for a Hallmark Ornament-of-the-year. I ended up buying a swimsuit for next summer. The sun was shining when I entered the store.' When I left, it was snowing. Even the weather was playing the "everything-at-once" game!

I can remember anticipating Thanksgiving. And when it was behind us, beginning to look forward to Christmas. When I was a child, the tree didn't even go up until Christmas Eve.

The kaleidoscope of celebrations confuses me. I'm a simple person. At mealtime, I like the full taste of one item at a time, not the potatoes-peas-pork chop all in one big mouthful. I like one celebration at a time. The overlap of holidays dulls the joyous anticipation of each one. Every taste offers its own delight, every holiday its own excitement.

But, alas, in our department store world, I fully expect, some day, to see a life size manger scene lighted by a string of orange pumpkins, with a big turkey standing in front of the sheep and the cow.

# 53.

We had a paper on the wall that went up the first day of October every year. It had a space for each member of the family to write in a date ... their guess of the first snowfall of the year. The one who guessed the nearest was the honored member of the family the next day. It was a like having an extra birthday without counting it as being a year older ... an extra Holiday for the family ... snow white cake and candles and all!

Sometimes it would be as early as October; sometimes not until December. There was the anticipation of being the one to see the first snowflake, though it really wasn't a big deal who won; it was a family fun time, a way of welcoming the Season that melted in with the preparations for Thanksgiving and Christmas and extended the "Holidays" even a bit longer.

Holidays are, after all, when you decide to have them, and what you decide to celebrate on those days. It might be the day you got your driver's license ... or contracted for your house ... or the first anniversary of your knee surgery. I've celebrated them all. They're like landmarks of your life.

Sometimes we like to play the game and get a bit fanciful. If you read Chase's Directory of Holidays, you'll discover that February 11 is "Don't Cry Over Spilt Milk" Day. December 17 is "National Chocolate Covered Anything" Day. August 13 is "National Left Hander's" Day, and March 26 is "Make Up Your Own Holiday" Day.

Holidays, times of remembrance, calendar a place for the special things in our lives, lest their meaning be lost in daily routines. Life would not be complete without pausing to give thanks for the harvest, for instance, or to celebrate the high moments of our Faith. Holidays are a unique way of combining the spirit of joy with the spirit of reverence, both of which are an essential part of our lives.

Happy Holidays!

# 54.

Every place I have ever worked, there have been first-day learnings. Some of these have been just getting acquainted with the job. Some have been like little initiations on the part of employees welcoming a "new man."

While I was in school, I took a part-time position as an orderly in the local hospital. My initial assignment was to take temperatures in the Men's Ward. I was instructed to clean the thermometers thoroughly after each use. I had always thought of hot water as the best cleanser, so I dutifully held the thermometer under very hot running water. Of course, the mercury blew right out the end. The Nurse was standing by, smiled and handed me a new thermometer and a bottle of alcohol.

But I wasn't through learning yet. My next task was to "prep" a man for surgery the next morning. I knew how to use a razor, so this was easy. However, I had now learned a new respect for alcohol so I thought I'd do it right this time and decided to wipe down the newly shaved area with a cotton pad soaked in alcohol. He hit the ceiling! I learned that alcohol wasn't for everything.

After he calmed down, he took a deep breath and said, "You're new here, aren't you?" Since he wasn't seriously hurt, I apologized and we could laugh about it. In the week or more that I knew him, I gave him extra care each day, and we became good friends. As a matter of fact, I learned, in that hospital, that there is a unique kind of bonding between those caring and those cared for. But this was a special relationship. We talked of many things, personal things that men could share.

One day, when I went in, he had been discharged. I never saw him again, but he had left for me a packet of poems that he had written while in the hospital. They weren't classic by literary standards, but they were a very personal gift of himself and I still have them among my treasures. And it is with a smile and a deep appreciation of a brief but unforgettable friendship that I think of him every time I pick up a bottle of alcohol.

# 55.

If I heard it once, I heard it 100 times, "Get your elbows off the table!" Like all children, I went through the growing process of learning to use my hands and feet ... and elbows ... without being clumsy. Elbows can cause accidents if you're not careful, or even be weapons when working your way through a crowd, but I never could see why the comfortable feeling of resting my elbows on the table was socially unacceptable.

Isn't it strange that we have a greater appreciation for things when we begin to lose them! As I grow older and don't flex as easily as I used to, I become increasingly aware of the importance of joints. I need my hands for gripping, my knees for walking, my shoulders for reaching and lifting. But elbows have uses even beyond the physical. While they are necessary for such activities as driving, combing my hair, and lifting food to my mouth, they often seem, also, to be an essential part of talking and thinking.

As a child, I remember watching adults lean on their elbows in spirited conversation. It helped them emphasize what they were saying. I remember my Dad, elbows on his knees, clasped hands under his chin, deep in thought. Also, how could you read the newspaper without your elbows to adjust the proper distance from your eyes?

At breakfast, one morning, I decided it would be fun to list all the ways I could think of that we use our elbows. The long list I came up with assured me that elbows are indeed a pretty important part of our lives. I laid the list aside and headed for the kitchen and suddenly realized I had missed one important elbow function. My hands full of dishes, I had automatically flicked out the dining room light ... with my elbow.

# 56.

When the American Eagle was chosen as our national symbol, it was in spite of the urging of Ben Franklin that the Turkey should have that honored place. At least the turkey found its place of honor as a national bird on our Thanksgiving tables and has become an established American food custom along with pumpkin pie.

Every country or culture has its food specialties. Pasta made its way to America with the Italian immigrants. The Germans introduced us to Sauerbraten. Irish stew and corned beef and cabbage are traditional dishes for the followers of Saint Patrick. If you've been in Arab countries, you know about sour goat's milk.

My father came to this country from England when he was 16. Even at that young age, he brought with him many of the old country tastes, which became standard fare at our family table. My mother, not English, but a devoted wife, must have steeled herself to prepare some of those foods.

When butcher shops were really meat markets, you could purchase any part of an animal that you wished. I can hardly get anyone to listen to me today when I try to explain how delicious calves' brains and scrambled eggs are, but for us they were a great breakfast treat.

The prize delicacy, for us kids, was a whole sheep's head. It made a wonderful dinner, but aside from that, my 3 brothers and I fought over the skull. The teeth made great "Tom Sawyer"-type pocket junk. We used the eyes like marbles.

The thing I really prized in my growing up years, however, was the traditional English Plum Pudding. We never seemed to have any "spare" money, but somehow the ingredients were accumulated bit by bit through the year.

The pudding itself, a Christmas tradition, had to be

prepared weeks ahead in order to be ripe, or cured (I never did understand what that meant). The only alcohol we ever had in our house was a bottle of brandy carefully stored on the pantry shelf to pour over the pudding on Christmas day. It had to be torched and served flaming to be authentic. That made the pudding exciting as well as delicious.

I enjoy celebrations with their special foods. I love birthday cakes, and I've enjoyed many, but not one could hold a candle to the ceremonial carrying in of those flaming English Christmas Plum Puddings.

# 57.

The old folks used to call it "set in his ways." I always liked the expression "stuck in a rut." That's what habits can do to you. As a boy, I was often told, "You've got a bad habit of...." or, "You've got to break the habit of...." I've long since forgotten what most of those bad habits were. A few, I remember; things like "picking your nose," "leaving the screen door open," "wiping your hands on your sleeve." Actually, I was pretty well grown up before I realized that not all habits are "bad," just the ones that annoyed your mother or father.

Habits are funny. With a well-established habit, the memory track triggers the action, and you don't even have to think. You brake for a red light; you've done it many times before. You lock the doors at night; that's routine. You fill the teakettle before you put it on the stove (and turn on the burner); that's automatic. Some of us click on the remote, turn on the TV and then hardly pay attention to it; that's habit.

Our lives are full of actions that have been grooved in our brain, and it's panic if there's an interruption. House and car keys are the worst offenders. How many times have you said, " ... but I know I left them **right here where I always do.**"

It takes discipline to break a habit. Oh, I can turn off the TV... if I think of it!

But I've had to train myself to substitute a napkin for a sleeve. It is possible to establish new habits. Repetition is the key. Come to think of it, even celebrating birthdays, year after year, can become a habit. Now there's a habit I'd like to keep ... as long as I can!

# 58.

    I'm working at the fine art of waiting! I find the doctor's office is my best lab for practicing. My appointment is scheduled for 1 pm. When I arrive, there are 6 persons already there. I figure an average of 30 minutes waiting time for each patient, and I think, "I could come back in 3 hours." No, I'd better wait in case there are papers for me to fill out. I select a seat. The others are staring at me, threateningly, lest I be called before they are. I try to be interested in an old magazine, but my eyes repeatedly return to my watch.

    Grocery stores are a kind of arena. This is not practice; this is the real thing, the battle of grocery carts! I have 8 items. The fast aisle says "7 items or less" The person ahead of me has an overflowing cart. I don't mean to watch, but I do, as she sets each item on the conveyor. I pass the time by imagining which items she'll be preparing for supper, wondering who the candy is for, fantasizing what the items reveal about who and how many are in her family. I turn for possible pleasantries with the man behind me, but he is already talking with the man behind him. I mentally total the prices on what I'm buying. I like to confuse the cashier by having the right amount ready. I'm off by 4 cents, but it was a diversion, anyway.

    Buses are frustrating. They are always a few minutes late but always drive up just as I unfold my newspaper.

    I find restaurants, however, are academies for learning how to wait. After I've been seated and taken note of all the decorations on the walls and ceiling, the waiter gets to my table with a menu. I quickly order the pork chops. Now, another time of waiting, but I don't mind, I fill this time anticipating my favorite meal. Eventually the waiter returns, but empty-handed. "Sorry," he says, "we're out of pork chops." Disappointed, I take undue time searching the menu for something else, but I appreciate the waiter's now waiting for me, graciously.

# 59.

A hundred years ago (1897, to be exact), an editorial in the New York Sun assured an 8 year old Virginia that "There is a Santa Claus." It was a classic statement of faith; and some lines are gems of inspiration:

> *"Alas! how dreary would be the world if there were no Santa Claus! ... There would be no childlike faith then, no poetry, no romance to make tolerable this existence ... The most real things in the world are those that neither children nor men can see."*

I have no problem with Santa at Christmas, side by side with the story of the Babe in the Manger, as long as we don't try to put them both in the same manger! Santa Claus emerges from the story of St. Nicholas, who was also beloved for his generosity. And while we must be careful that Santa Claus not become "God," it is true that the nature of God is often revealed in stories of men and women (and Santa Claus?) who personify love and faithfulness and untiring service to humankind ... and especially in that warm, wonderful affection for children that keeps the world delightfully human. The "romance" quoted above in the letter to Virginia is the fascinating ability of children to put flesh on creative imagination.

I only regret that, along with so many other good things, we have commercialized Santa Claus. He is on the street in all sizes and shapes and ill-fitting suits and beards. He is in the stores, asking but not hearing or caring what Johnny wants for Christmas, a jolly salesman who will have his picture taken with your child for a price. The effect is sometimes more disillusioning than affirming for children. They see through the sham, redeemed only by their own instinctive ability to pretend.

The Christmas gift that children need and basically want, and will treasure for life, is to savor the poetry and romance in the story of Christmas, even in the midst of all the hype.

# 60.

Time was, when Christmas eve saw families gathered around a Christmas tree decorated with lighted candles. It was a risky thing to do, but during the time the candles were burning, the children were carefully kept from the tree at a table of hot cocoa and cookies. This was family time, singing the old carols in the soft light and watching the candle flames flicker like stars through the branches. It was all so beautiful! Our homes are safer now, with strings of electric lights on the tree, but we still love the glow of the candles and find other ways to enjoy them.

We accent our holiday homes with colored candles and welcome guests to a friendly candlelight atmosphere. Candles are symbols of hospitality. They are also symbols of celebration and of the sacred times of life. Candles at a wedding reflect the solemn uniting of two persons as they pledge their lives to each other in love. Our services of worship include candles on the altar to represent the illumination of our lives by the presence of God.

The celebration of Christmas and Hannukah and Kwanzaa are all variations of the Festival of Lights. It is in this season of long nights, that we light our candles as if to dispel the darkness, physically and spiritually. Let the Holiday stores set themselves ablaze in artificial light, it is the quiet mystery of the blue and yellow candle flame that carries the message of the wonder and peace of the holy season.

How wonderful, we think, if we could keep this glorious season all year long. But seasons run their course. We put away the tree and the decorations, but not the candles. They stay! Candles are season-less! The old year comes to a close, but the New Year beckons us to bring our candles and join the celebration, where they now serve as symbols of new beginnings, equally as well as of old traditions.

# 61.

Christmas wouldn't have been Christmas without the standard 3 packages under the tree ... new underwear, new socks, and a new toy or game. And, of course, the stocking with nuts and candy and an orange in the toe.

I always hoped it would be a new game. A toy could be interesting for the moment, but a game could be played over and over again. In fact, if each of us kids got a different game, there would be four of them to play. Pretty good variety in those days before television!

We always decorated the tree with the ornaments left over from past years. We might add popcorn strings or paper cut-outs, but we knew every colored ball that came out of the box. I never knew where those old ornaments had come from. They were part of Christmas and were timeless, like Christmas itself.

In those days, having anything new was a very special occasion. New shoes were not just for wearing. They were something you showed off to everyone you knew. Even though we knew, year after year, that there would be the standard 3 packages, there was still an element of excitement about it. These were *new* underwear and socks. That was enough to make it Christmas.

Today, I pick up what I need, or think I need, throughout the year. And so I have two drawers filled with old socks and no room to stuff in any more. Why do I have so many? For one thing, I'm saving several single socks hoping the mate will show up someday. But that doesn't explain the over-supply.

Am I missing the fun of Christmas ... the fun of looking forward all year to those simple packages under the tree? I think that, since I dislike shopping anyway, I may leave some of the basics to Santa this year. It would be good for me to go back to the days of an empty drawer and know again the joy of "something new" at Christmas ... especially if it's underwear and socks!

# 62.

It's a wonderful word, "anyway"! And it's an attitude that gets me through many a difficult situation. I learned the word from a little boy who had lost, in a game with a couple of other boys, a whole bag of marbles ... except one. I thought he'd be crying as he walked away, but instead, I heard him say, "Anyway, I've still got one."

More than that, he had no anger against the other boys. They had won fairly in a game and, anyway, it was his own decision to join the game. They were still his friends. And anyway, there would be another game, and he still had his "shooter."

I thought that was a pretty mature attitude, to focus on what he still had, not on what he had lost, and to think ahead to the future when, anyway, he would have another chance.

We experience many losses as we grow older. It would be so easy to surrender and drown in our self-pity, or even grow angry and turn away our friends. That's when we have to call on the "anyway" strategy:

"I can't walk as well as I used to, but I'm going to the lunch at the Senior Center anyway, to be with my friends."

"My grandson is getting a merit badge at Scouts tonight. I'm exhausted from a hard day at work but I'll be there, anyway."

"I don't have time, but I'll stop by the hospital, anyway, to say hello after my friend's surgery."

And all of those sentences end with, "and I'm glad I did."

It may be a simple tool, but I find it's a great help for keeping myself in line. Anyway, I get a lot more pleasure out of life, keeping "anyway" handy.